what is near

kay syrad

Cinnamon Press
:: small miracles from distinctive voices ::

Published by Cinnamon Press
www.cinnamonpress.com

The right of Kay Syrad to be identified as author of this work has been asserted by her in accordance with the Copyright, Designs and Patent Act, 1988. © 2021, Kay Syrad

ISBN 978-1-78864-113-5

British Library Cataloguing in Publication Data. A CIP record for this book can be obtained from the British Library.

Designed and typeset in Bodoni by Cinnamon Press. Cover design by Adam Craig.

Cinnamon Press is represented by Inpress

Acknowledgements

Thanks are due to the editors of the following journals and anthologies, in which some of the poems in this collection or a version of them were first published: *Invasive* (Elephant Press, 2019), *Wetland Eco-Body* (Elephant Press, 2020), *Chichester Festival Anthology* (2019 and 2020), *t/here* (East Port Editions, 2019) and the journals *Fenland Reed, Tears in the Fence, Molly Bloom* and *Finished Creatures*.

I am indebted to Jan Fortune at Cinnamon Press, to Chris Drury and my family, and the poets at my two regular workshop groups. Special thanks to Peter Abbs, Lisa Dart, Kim Lasky and Clare Whistler for their perceptive close readings and encouragement.

Contents

for Betty
her future

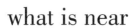

what is near

moss

after the great drought
moss will remember

breathing is disturbed

would that human
   force was only a needle's
push through tight
   weave
     and the only clock
a bell when
   bell-casting was hard and
     beautiful and
treasured

what is precious now

there's talk of a common
   pulsing
     a new cleaving of us
and other

non-attachment theory

the thing about moss
    apart from its greenness

            the low winter sun warmed our faces
            as we stepped over fallen branches

is that it has no roots
    only rhizoids

            in the forest   newly green-warmed
            by the moss and green rushes

single cell organs
    slim as hair or thread

            among the rust-grey leaves the colour
            of roe deer   muntjacs

that nestle beneath
    the leaf-rows or spirals

            our hands on the moss   so yielding   so wet
            so flamboyant and bright

anchoring them
    to tree or rock   absorbing

            still fresh   after 540 million years
            to the taste of this dewy air

and carrying water slow
    along their filaments

reaching for the moss

when my hand is on moss
what is inside is brought to the periphery

I have fingers   a palm   a thumb (though less so)
I do not know what my fingers register
in their own language
so I call the sensations *ah   tickle   brush*
impermanence fills my head—

and with that small knowledge
something is quieted

I will be quiet

I am quiet with moss
I look through a magnifier
I reach
and moss reaches
it unfurls for moisture
—can I reach the moss   no
this is the dread

I am between sense
and explanation
can't remember what to do
about that dread
perhaps make room for it
as a guest   a message
it says   this feeling
is a golden feeling   the body
in waves   rolls
organs lifting

yet   still I cannot reach
must remain—
like the boundary layer—
between host-surface
and moss

coming to the periphery

the skin opens to colour   to colour green   and stays open for
    texture   for feel   the feel of green   for waterdrops
skin merging with green   hand cupping green   always the
    hand curve-cupping   not only the green but the tending
of the green   meeting the moss's yielding   with skin effort
    breath effort   heart effort   it was a simple walk   the line
of beech trees   hornbeams   close-circled by moss on the path
    the sinew   muscularity of the beech bark   one one one one
a border-boundary *boeke   buche   buch   boc*   not understanding
    never   only long-longing   now moss is the yearning
extending   to be reached-with   though hope is not a given
    coming towards by means   in distance   or nearness

t/here

it began   with a lone dunlin
that interest in   egress and ingress
inrush   exile —
its long beak   making a mirrored arc
silent   on the shallow water
a two-bird   born in Siberia   wintering
here   divided by time and breath —

and continues with names   ox-bird
plover's page   sea-snipe and stint
and   the black streak on its back   dun wings
breast-white   tapering again to   black
the females rising first   to fly
over   'waters of the great deep'
to reach   arrive — again

the curlew has   sensors
nerve endings held   at the tip
of a hook bill that it drives   into the sand's
mudding to seize   shrimps and worms
and in its jaw   Herbst's corpuscles
to detect   the vibrations
of crustaceans moving   below sight

all is so   finely calibrated
so highly evolved   that my own sensors —
concentrated in   eye or   mouth
or   mind — fail   fall through sand's
quickening   into the realms
of transferral   translation
and tremble   at the   magnitude

the figure   arrives
keeps arriving
this time with   flowers
figure arrives
with flowers   for the grave
enters

retreats
without   flowers
a time   without flowers
the figure retreats
arrives   and retreats
with   or   without flowers

they (   )

were standing

they were standing

in a
straight   line

when the tide

when
the   tide

came   in

they (   )

were standing

when

they (   ) were

not

(   ) rescued

every day   I leave my conscience
there   in order to be   here

night and day   I leave what I know is
wrong   outside   over there
above or below   the horizon

each morning and afternoon   I notice

flecks   cuts   and unexplained   light-glare

try to accept that   sea   and sky
can be   indistinguishable   even lush
for the eyes

but   the remembering   implores
                              clarity

dear M   it was me who bought your tulip painting
I named it 'Iranian tulips' knowing only that little
about you   I coveted it at once   the tulips were birds
that sang straight into my heart   they flew out
of the canvas   opening and closing   arriving closed
perhaps but with a promise   an expectation
of their outer petals laying away   yellows   reds
orange   and the stems so dark and definite

I saw a generosity in the design   an intensity
noticed the light blue between these stems   the lilac
between the others   how light emanates
from the flowers' tips   the shading   and the criss-
crossing of the leaves   the boldness of the lines
and I greet you   I greet you   I greet you

a true horizon they say   is theoretical
although it surrounds you   and its centre
is below you   below sea level
are you also below sea level   and the offing
(the sea closest to the horizon line)
is about three miles away depending on
how tall you are   or if you're on a hill
or in fear   or alone   and also on atmospheric

refraction   here   you have salt marsh   mud flats
twenty thousand birds in form   who know
how the sun   moves on a horizontal plane
who know the significance of   shadows
the position   of stars   know that insects trees
flowers   and mosses   are migrating too

no   not

we took a path   away from   the heart
that day   we're taking that path
every day

no not

they said no   not

    they also said no   not

in different north south east west
        at time

all in the forest said
                      no   not

but the fires are a lie
              the president said

white and grey smoke rising   is
      a lie
              village fallen   a lie   charred pasture   a lie

quiruyu huapa tree   chunchu tree   burning   a lie

1,000 fires   a lie
      7,600 fires   a lie
                                     29,307 fires
                    30,900 fires
      a burning lie

every living form exquisitely evolved

                one million years   500 million years

            epiphytic cactus   shangu   spotwinged antbird burning

collared anteater   white-lipped peccary   burning

all symbiosis burning

           guan   jaguar   ucucha
                         burning

whiplash beetle   crab-eating racoon   burning burning

our

       their

all in the forest asked
                    no   not

       also no and not

in the river form   stream form

       in the leaf form   bird form

in the

others said
       others said fire said said fire   said fire   said fire said fire

burn the whole air

no

now we hardly ever

because nothing
happens now
and

now we hardly ever

gather
harvest   store
(when to gather)
share
(when to harvest)
(how to store)
(share)
loosening
(all grown over)
bonds
(~~share~~)
loosing
(

long denial

[...once]   all the loved seasons
          were shimmering within us
    drawing us forward

[...but you know, even
the]   cui-ui fish
          low-feeding in the black lake
    need water to spawn

[...and as I already
said]   nothing happens now
          happen was then   in slow time
    in spirit time

[...and]   even when full-with
          bloom-with damselfly sun-scent
    the wind bears the cries

[...ok, so]   how near must a thing
          be for us to feel be felt
    what sensation is longed for

[...go on]   take this long feather
          our face neck throat palm can feel
    also our thumb-joint

[...or]   shape a small bowl-nest
          of birch bark papers surround
    loosely with twigs light

[...because]   every small thing
          is dense with complexity
    markings splits spurs spikes

[…]　　　every small or large
　　　　　　　thing is thinking　　making signs
　　　　　　gall wasps —　　　　　　fungi
[…for example, can
　　　command]　　the carpenter ant
　　　　　　　　　　to climb a much-too-tall stem
　　　　　　　and bite it at noon

[…to release nutrients
　　　and]　　that moss in the cleft
　　　　　　　　of the tall beech is etched in
　　　　　　solidarity

[…also]　　endurance　can speak
　　　　　　　　in turtle years or redwood
　　　　　　and patterns whisper

[…so come on, let's]　　gather seeds　　observe
　　　　　　　　　　tenderly a petal's stripes
　　　　　　　its intense purple

[…because soon]　　*they will slip from us*
　　　　　　　　　will flourish
　　　　　　　without us

33

out   there

caught by the sun   the fly zigzags   darts
disappears   another or the same fly appears
darts   disappears   the beech branches grow out
horizontally seeking light   the leaves bright green
and shadowing   some yellow   the oak
hooshes in its high canopy   the wind
the sound   the green   the yellow

in   here

shame happens and a proxy shame happens
the feeling filters down through organs
tissue   as if woven on a loom   as if the body
is a loom and shame the warp the weft

out   here

is where I am   in the all-ish vastness of wrong acts
a half-thought   a said/unsaid   the buzzing
isn't continuous but pulses at intervals   re-charging
in the (de) forest   in the parched soil

meanwhile   I barely know what grass is

there are daisies in the grass all summer
so many   in autumn worm mounds so
many   in winter I lose interest in the grass
I forget the grass   wrest only its easy green

I also forget the names of soundless trees
shrubs flowers   as if they are mine to forget
I can neither match the songs of birds to feather
nor even say this call is avian or mammal

or human   I study   trace   photograph
join an observation group   note habitat
mythology symbol   yet still I barely know

what grass is   even when you say *family Poaceae*
say   blade node stem culm stolon tiller sheath
auricle and ligule   instead of lawn or turf

chrysalis
Pieris brassicae

I can only assume that
in a very long   non-linear
to the wall by silk pads
we emerge   perhaps
white shell   a radiant
inscriptions   the meaning

we have all been trapped
pupation   girdled
and tiny hooks   when
we will leave behind an ivory-
tracery of silver-gold-and-black
of exquisite

what is near

leaf composure

how strong the petiole
holds while all the lobe-lost lacings fall
free to lacings fall (ah)
this one lichening dots of white here
here   a filament a fibril drawing in fixing
—and another one
open arc   exposure   shush the soft tearing
of the veins veining curve to lost apex

the beauty of this threads-to-nowhere
un-life-ing   re-life-ing
so delicate neither palm nor fingertip
only eye
can register the weight

attitude

standing

      vertical
        in the face of
            in   responsibility

      here   long-seeing is currency

 and order:
  muscular apple branches   plum leaves (over)
                           yellow oak leaves   white sky

          there is air where the seeing is

      [can see   be seen]

sitting

      entitlement
            above   without effort

slow noticing
      desire to touch alter re-arrange
remove
           ivy   leather-strong

pine fronds ginger to verdant   from death to life or life to death

      [can leave   can take]

kneeling

     is serious
             finds texture before   colour   probably

pine seed casing   two raised lines down its flank   a shield

     [can see   hear   arrives with effort]

lying down

     listening   as if to scent

               pine needles   earth-grass

       head   palms   fingers

     [can touch   be touched]

f eath er

.

        it is
dark   this path   these oaks   hornbeams
        and the buzzard so human-close
wingspan wider
        than our eyes' range
   slow down-swoop
            held for a moment
        in a shouldered arc

next day I hear him in the sky   *peeioo*   *peeioo*

        and today hold a perfect tail feather
its downy tines and filoplumes
        once webbing
   the feather in place in the bird-body
            expertly

-

all is level here

Pevensey Levels

grazed fen-swamp
tussock-edged ditches
flat water grasses
this day   one thousand years

>the five-leaved pondweed
>shining pondweed
>sharp-leaved pondweed
>water plantains

black cattle
hooves deep-slipped in mud

what is rare

>water violet and bladderwort
>cuckoo flower
>water lilies small as a coin

light is low   sometimes a thought
of brightening

>tall reeds   bur reed
>tall fen
>yellow irises

>reed bunting   reed warbler
>sedge warbler   cetti's warbler
>yellow wagtail

will you claim   re-claim this land
it is temporal   adaptive

>herbivorous beetle
>great silver water beetle
>diving beetle   red beetle

so much is rare

      hairy hawker spider
      fen-raft spider the size of your palm
      eats fish
      nursery web spider

clamour of wind   claim of wind
levelling   levering

dredge   mussel shells
mud-coils

nitrates or phosphates
shining pools
on the marshy grass

      tench   perch   pike
      rudd need weedy ditches
      frogs   water shrews
      harvest mice nesting in the reeds

all is rare

      little whirlpool ramshorn snail
      shining ramshorn snail
      large-mouthed valve snail
      false orb pea mussel

      yellow loose strife
      and the yellow loose strife bee
      excites the yellow flower pollen
      takes the oil for its bee-nest

rare

       hairy dragonfly
       variable damselfly
       13-spot ladybird

forty per cent fewer
only 15-20 pairs left
eighty per cent lower
only two pairs left

sheep beneath
the floating pennywort

lichen think-me

found the fallen tangle
   of dry powdered
prehistorical antler tentacular
   silverwhite and greysilver
pair-obligate sprig-lobes
   on the mossy slope
that day when green was alight
   in the brown lake and the trees
were waving water-mountains

   made a tiny exhibition
from the out-mind tiny billion-year-old
   biospheres   the slow-grow
one-millimetre-a-year
   algal-cyanobacterial-fungal-yeast-
lichenising symbionts   not
   one thing but a ceaseless song
of reciprocity

   but with texture preferences
smooth young hazel   a rough oak
   and forest work to do
sheltering mites and moth larvae
   holding and releasing   in time
toxins rain or dew

   and so we breathe

sentience

word   I want to know where that word is now
          the person who went to work one day   Whitehall   picked up
a latte on the way   carried it   burning their fingers   across St
James Park   past the swans and ducks and people   paused at the
bridge and sipped at the coffee   heard the morning birdsong   saw a
stealthy cat and seven dogs   glimpsed the horses on parade on the
Mall   their long shining backs   the sound of their hooves   threw
their cup in a waste bin   walked swiftly in   greeted Security   swiped
their ID card   in through the double doors the ones with old wood
and small glass panes   sat down at their desk   remembered the
meeting   looked out the notes   opened the computer   scrolled down
the EU Repeal Bill   clicked on find   found the word sentient
pressed delete   and again   allowed Microsoft to search the doc   from
the beginning   from the end   one stray   delete
          outside   a pigeon burbled on the ledge   the traffic screeched
voices carried
I signed a petition to reinstate the word sentience   *I signed a*
petition to reinstate   reinforce the word sentience *and that day I*
disturbed a one millimeter black spider on the windowsill   eased it
outside on a butter knife   was bitten on the back of the leg by a gnat
remembered Kafka's story of Red Peter who reported to the Academy
on how he   an ape   learned human ways
          earlier   the bees were shimmying on pink flowers   the
yellow roses were rising from a thinning bush   the berries were red
red in the guelder rose   the squirrels were flying   crack crack crack
acorns twigs   a nuthatch upside down at the birdfeeder
          voices carried

re-forestation with exotic species

[...] is practiced with eucalyptus   pine   silver wattle
(an acacia)   silky oak   and paperbark

a woman or a man named these 'exotic' species

someone said 'ah   silky oak'   tongue sliding
behind the teeth for the 'l'   pressure for the 'k's

someone said 'hmmm   silver wattle'   bringing
the acacia into the known   to discover it   to love it

another said 'this   this is paperbark'   and knew
afresh the feel   texture   the way of paper

and all these are being carried back to the forest
to be re-said   *(forest)*   re-heard in their wordings

sentience (ii)

the silence of the cat's body
    is in the fur hinges of its hind legs
a low feather-weight advance
    all of evolution in the stealth

the duck leads her remaining ducklings
    to the fence   waits as we unbolt
the stiff gate   eases out   along the road
    away —

days later we hear a mournful crying
    the duck and drake together
balancing on the level hedge

calling for the ducklings lost   or dead
    and the next morning   the next   and next
imprinted then on all the mornings

mourning the wild glory

turn your palm to face you
and move your wrist
in slow circles to the left
to know how tenderly
how imperceptibly the tendrils
wreathe their light-host

and when you know this
vow   pledge
promise

unceasing vigilance

moss (ii)

dew / mist

(i)

moss
    awning for the tree roots
clings   reaches   lifts
    on free air
        and air is a tunnel
    for dew
the air carries the light dew
    towards the fronds
        to the frond tips
    where all the parts are gathering

I carry the air in my heart
    heart fronds

(ii)

mist is usually   over there
    creating unformed things
that could be love   or chance

mist is usually at the beginning
    offering tone   and mood
releasing shapes   white scored
    pewter

but mist   descending out
    of light   is noticed by the one celled
moss leaves   that unfurl   spread
    adjust their angles

concatenation

I place the moss sample in a low dish with water
   expect to feel its vibrational rhythm as it drinks
I wait I want the moss to take up the water faster
   I turn it upside down   drink! dear moss I say
though I know you work slowly I turn you back
   the right way up   wait brooding for your dry coils
to bloom and blossom   still no! perhaps I cannot
   understand what waiting is will never recognise
this other's pulse   yet I am near I dab dab you
   in the shallow water and feel   oh despair!
for our own barrenness   our lost textures   I will
   touch this paper   light-shadow   as my fingers
brush apprehend the creamy grain   the moss
   is fluffing up now   it is my pet!   what is going on

54

boundary layer

we imagine we are entire
                smooth   and continuous   and something of us
                   edges   or surges towards
                           but only as far as   the lovely
           membrane
and yet

        what membrane is it that admits water   air   dust
            that releases sounds   gases   terror

can we sense the interior   what realm is this
            but one of   contraction and   expansion
                        striated muscles   the raging

teeming viscera
                that   flesh   does not describe

block

when I foundered   met resistance to the poems
I wondered if I could draw the moss   bought
graphite and coloured pencils   sketch book
I could not draw the moss

then I thought to show those luscious colours
in short green lines   square stack of lines
to precede each poem   a path into each
I have drawn no lines

I re read my notes   turns out I already knew
such lines mean   hopelessness   or shame
the colour of shame is dark blue
with red   the colour

of hope is green after 7 days of continuous rain
for example   but oh   what is *any*thing   loss
reach   the considerable reach of loss
its tendered flesh

I will not go now

to the moss forests to
Puzzlewood Forest
the Forest of Dean to
Wistman's Wood on
Dartmoor on the slopes of
the West Dart River a
high oakwood one of
only three such woods
and haunted

I will not go now to
the moss forest
at Loch Awe in the
north of Scotland nor to
the Atlantic Woodland at
Ariundle where
ancient oak and ash and
birch and hazel call to
each other among the
five hundred of mosses and
ferns and liverworts and
lichens the

spotty featherwort prickly
featherwort also
deceptive featherwort
toothed pouncewort
yellow speckle belly and

Wilson's filmy fern
some
unknown elsewhere

becoming vegetal

moss waits   patiently   for rain
  and before it arrives   draws down
the rain's breath   tilting for light

here is the monk   eight years dead
  raised up a little from the ground
his body now a pelt of dark moss

  living-dying   a slow un-being

the tiny reach between each green tendril
  swells to stay the viscous water
and every leaf's surface resists the sun's pull

  ah   the close effort of transmutation

let it give us feeling   beyond origin
  to say   life-death *is* beauty
spore   light   cell   molecule

to behold   a monk   robes once saffron
  waiting patiently   as if for rain

notes

'breathing is disturbed' is a phrase from Frank Berardi's *Breathing, Chaos and Poetry* (2019).

't/here' — an inquiry into human and non-human migration, was originally part of a collaboration with artist Chris Drury and published in a limited edition by East Port (2019) with images from Drury's Horizon Line Chamber at Sunderland Point, Lancashire.

'they' were 21 young people mostly from Fujian and Shanghai in China who were working as cockle pickers when they were drowned at Morecambe Bay on 5th February 2004.

'the figure arrives' — in the 18th century, Sunderland Point was an out-port for Lancaster, where ships holding enslaved people, cotton, tobacco and sugar, could unload or wait before moving on to the main docks. The Port of Lancaster was part of the 'slavery triangle', with enslaved people transported through the 'Middle Passage' between Africa and America. On the peninsula lies the grave of a young man thought to be the African servant of the ship's captain, and who died in the village c. 1736.

're-forestation with exotic species' — the title and quotation at the start of this poem are adapted from a footnote in Donna Haraway's *Staying with the Trouble: Making Kin in the Chthulucene* (2016), Duke University Press.

'sentience' — Franz Kafka, 'A Report to the Academy' (1917)

'I will not go now' was written during the first UK Covid-19 lockdown 2020